ABDO
Publishing Company

Yoga

MOVE
YOUR
BODY

A Kid's Guide to Fitness

A Buddy Book by **Sarah Tieck**

VISIT US AT
www.abdopublishing.com

Published by ABDO Publishing Company, PO Box 398166, Minneapolis, MN 55439.

Printed in the United States of America, North Mankato, Minnesota.
102012
012013

 PRINTED ON RECYCLED PAPER

Coordinating Series Editor: Rochelle Baltzer
Contributing Editors: Stephanie Hedlund, Marcia Zappa
Graphic Design: Jenny Christensen
Cover Photograph: *iStockphoto*: ©iStockphoto.com/blackwaterimages.
Interior Photographs/Illustrations: *Eighth Street Studio* (p. 26); *Getty Images*: Angela Coppola (p. 9), Jamie Grill (p. 17), Zia Soleil (p. 5), Julie Toy (pp. 25, 29); *Glow Images*: Ira Block/National Geographic Image Collection (p. 15); *iStockphoto*: ©iStockphoto.com/Blend_Images (p. 23), ©iStockphoto.com/Jmichl (p. 19), ©iStockphoto.com/nicolesy (pp. 19, 21), ©iStockphoto.com/pixdeluxe (p. 7), ©iStockphoto.com/SochAnam (p. 9), ©iStockphoto.com/ultraF (p. 7); *Shutterstock*: Roi Brooks (p. 9), Deklofenak (p. 30), Rob Marmion (pp. 13, 26), Nuzza (p. 11); *Thinkstock*: Hemera (p. 13, 27), Keith Levit Photography (p. 29).

Library of Congress Cataloging-in-Publication Data

Tieck, Sarah, 1976-
  Yoga / Sarah Tieck.
     p. cm. -- (Move your body : a kid's guide to fitness)
  ISBN 978-1-61783-565-0 (hardcover)
 1. Yoga--Juvenile literature. I. Title.
 RA781.7.T53 2013
 613.7'046--dc23
                          2012032933

Table of Contents

Healthy Living

Your body is amazing! A healthy body helps you feel good and live well. In order to be healthy, you must take care of yourself. One way to do this is to move your body.

Regular movement gives you **energy** and makes you stronger. Many kinds of exercise can help you do this. One fun type of exercise is yoga! Let's learn more about yoga.

In a yoga class, people move their bodies into different positions. They also do breathing and mind exercises.

Yoga 101

To practice yoga, people move their bodies on mats. They must balance as they move into different poses. They also work to control their thoughts and breathing.

Yoga workouts can be long or short. They can also be easy or hard. Some people do yoga as part of a **spiritual** practice. Many others do it as a form of exercise.

People practice yoga alone or in groups. They do it at home, outside, or at a gym.

A yoga teacher is sometimes called a guru (GUR-oo). Yoga students may be called yogis (YOH-gees).

WORD OF MOUTH

WORD OF

MOUTH

Yoga poses are also called asanas (AH-suh-nuhs). They are combined for a complete workout.

There are many poses in yoga. Some are done while standing. Others are done while sitting or laying down. Poses build strength, stretch **muscles**, or help you relax. A yoga workout includes different types of poses.

Child's pose is a resting pose.

Downward-facing dog pose stretches the shoulders, hands, and legs.

Upward-facing dog pose stretches your chest and strengthens your arms.

Let's Get Physical

People exercise to stay fit. Regular exercise, such as yoga, helps you stay at a healthy body weight. It also helps prevent health problems later in life.

Yoga has many health benefits. It makes you more **flexible**. It also improves balance. Yoga makes some people feel calmer, too.

Crow pose helps improve balance and upper body strength. It is a challenging pose!

Yoga builds your **muscles**. Many common poses work your leg and arm muscles. And, you must use your abdominal and back muscles to balance.

Over time, your body gets stronger. Yoga poses may become easier. Then, you can do more **challenging** poses.

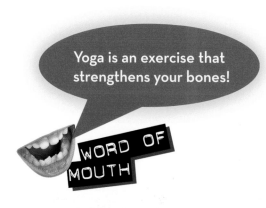

Yoga is an exercise that strengthens your bones!

WORD OF MOUTH

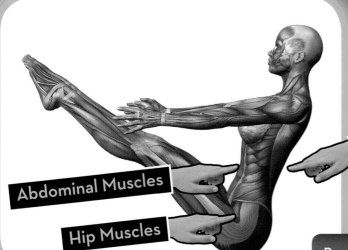

Back Muscles

Abdominal Muscles

Hip Muscles

Boat pose works your abdominal, back, and hip muscles.

Gearing Up

To do yoga, wear clothes that allow you to move freely. You should have bare feet. You need a special mat so your feet and hands won't slip. Yoga is often done in a quiet room. That way, people can listen to their breathing.

Certain tools help people do yoga. Blocks or straps help beginners do poses that they might not be **flexible** enough to do. These tools also help people stretch deeper or hold poses longer.

Blocks and straps can help people improve.

Play It Safe

Safety is important for yoga, especially as a beginner. First, make sure that you eat lightly before doing yoga. Also, choose a space that is not too hot or cold.

As you practice yoga, pay attention to how your body feels. If you are doing a difficult or new pose, move slowly. Stop if a pose hurts. Only do poses that are right for your body. And, avoid doing yoga if you are sick or hurt.

Some yoga movements require you to balance on one leg or even stand on your head!

WORD OF MOUTH

Practicing yoga on level ground is one way to stay safe. Also, ask your teacher how to change poses to make them simpler.

Many types of yoga are safe for beginners. Hatha and Iyengar yoga offer lighter movements.

Ashtanga, vinyasa, and power yoga use fast movements. Bikram yoga is also called hot yoga. It is done in a room that is often more than 100°F (38°C). These types are for people in good health and with experience.

 **How It Sounds**

hatha (HAHTH-uh)
Iyengar (ee-YEHNG-gahr)
ashtanga (ash-TAHNG-uh)
vinyasa (vihn-YAH-suh)
Bikram (BIHK-ram)

Eight-angle pose (*above*) and the supported headstand pose (*right*) are not for beginners.

Ready? Set? Go!

Before doing yoga, warm up with slow, easy movements. Pay attention to your thoughts and your breathing. This prepares your mind and body to work hard during exercise.

Many people end their yoga practice with relaxation. They lay down and close their eyes. After relaxation, they begin slowly moving their bodies again.

Corpse pose is for relaxing.

Look and Learn

For many people, yoga is more than just a workout. For some, it is a **spiritual** practice. They use poses and movements to learn about themselves. Many **Hindus** practice yoga to feel connected to a higher power.

Yoga can help you become calmer. It can also help you get to or stay at a healthy weight.

Take Care

Before you begin yoga, check that your mat is clean. Make sure that you have a clear, level space to move in.

It is important to do each pose correctly to avoid getting hurt. You can learn from a yoga teacher, book, or video. During a yoga pose, notice if you have any pain. If you do, then carefully come out of the pose.

Teachers can help improve your form. They may also help you deepen stretches.

Brain Food

How do you know if you are doing yoga hard enough to get a workout?

Many exercises work your heart and lungs. Yoga is usually a different type of workout. It helps you use your body weight to build strength.

Moving into poses and holding them works your muscles. You'll know you are working hard as your muscles get tired. And, the poses may get easier over time.

How are you supposed to breathe during yoga?

During yoga, breathe in and out through your nose. Keep your breath slow. It is important to pay attention to each breath. This helps calm your mind. It also makes movements easier.

What is the best way to eat for yoga?

It is best to eat very lightly before a yoga workout. A piece of fruit or some vegetables might be a good choice. Some yoga poses twist and bend your body. This may feel uncomfortable on a full stomach.

Choose to Move

Remember that yoga is a type of fitness that makes your body stronger. Fitness is an important part of a healthy life. Do yoga as often as you can. Each positive choice you make will help you stay healthy.

Over time, yoga may be something you do for fun and well-being!

29

HEALTHY BODY FILES

GROW STRONG

✔ Set a **goal** to improve your yoga skills. Take a class at a local gym or school to learn new poses.

✔ Time how long you can hold a pose. Then, see if you can hold it longer next time!

BODY FUEL

✔ Water plays an important part in helping your body build **muscle**. So, be sure to drink water before, during, and after yoga.

✔ Lean **proteins** such as chicken or low-fat milk help your muscles grow stronger. It is good to eat protein after a yoga workout.

STAY SAFE

✔ If you do yoga outdoors, wear sunscreen. This helps **protect** your skin.

✔ It's a good idea to get your own yoga mat. If you borrow one, be sure to clean it before and after you use it.

Important Words

challenging (CHA-luhn-jihng) testing one's strengths or abilities.

energy (EH-nuhr-jee) the power or ability to do things.

flexible able to bend or move easily.

goal something that a person works to reach or complete.

Hindu (HIHN-doo) a person who practices Hinduism, which is a religion from India.

lungs body parts that help the body breathe.

muscle (MUH-suhl) body tissue, or layers of cells, that helps move the body.

protect (pruh-TEHKT) to guard against harm or danger.

protein (PROH-teen) an important part of the diet of all animals.

spiritual of or relating to the spirit or soul instead of physical things.

Web Sites

To learn more about yoga, visit ABDO Publishing Company online. Web sites about yoga are featured on our Book Links page. These links are routinely monitored and updated to provide the most current information available.

www.abdopublishing.com

Index